Burnt Matches

Vol. 1

Maylee Curtis

The views and opinions expressed in this book are solely those of the author and do not reflect the views or opinions of Gatekeeper Press. Gatekeeper Press is not to be held responsible for and expressly disclaims responsibility of the content herein.

Burnt Matches

Published by Gatekeeper Press
2167 Stringtown Rd, Suite 109
Columbus, OH 43123-2989
www.GatekeeperPress.com

Copyright © 2022 by Maylee Curtis

All rights reserved. Neither this book, nor any parts within it may be sold or reproduced in any form or by any electronic or mechanical means, including information storage and retrieval systems, without permission in writing from the author. The only exception is by a reviewer, who may quote short excerpts in a review.

The cover design and editorial work for this book are entirely the product of the author. Gatekeeper Press did not participate in and is not responsible for any aspect of these elements.

Library of Congress Control Number: 2022942295

ISBN (paperback): 9781662930447
eISBN: 9781662930454

for

the handful of friends,

family,

the ones who picked up

this book,

and to the people behind it

but will never open it

and if she ever

                        fell in love with me,

i'd handle her delicately

like a lilac growing in the

desert heat

- m.c

I'm just a twenty year old girl

who likes girls

Contents

The Falling 2

The Goodbye 22

The Regret 40

The Falling

1

m.c

i told myself

"i'd never fall in love again"

but then

i found *her*

burnt matches

your lips were like honey

leaving the sweetness on my tongue

in need of more

m.c

two weeks ago

you caught me off guard pouring your tea

two weeks before that

i noticed you looking at me

two weeks later *you* kissed me

tracing your hands on my pant seams

creating art on your skin

hoping i'll see you again

two weeks you'll be gone

we won't think of one another

but maybe we will after two weeks

burnt matches

her body is art

and it speaks volumes with mine

m.c

they said,

"you could do better"

but who wants a digital copy of cleopatra

burnt matches

she had me at her fingertips

the moment

her skin arranged with mine

m.c

you looked at me

like the moon

looks at the stars

far away but worth looking at

burnt matches

and *she*,

she is the reason for my poetry

m.c

she's not the type to bring

your parents to

but the one you'll tell

strangers about

burnt matches

you touched parts of me

i didn't even know

existed

m.c

death begged me to follow it

but then

i met *her*

burnt matches

she was like rain on a sunny day

unexpected but beautiful

like coffee but not too sweet

that's the type of girl

you'd write about

forever

tell her

you love her from the deepest

parts of your

soul

tell her

you need her on the days

she isn't home

tell her

she's amazing when she is simply out of

control

burnt matches

and if we turn into an

"almost"

i hope the moon is not too late for us

in the upcoming orbit

m.c

i dare you to make

a poet love you

in other words

your existence will never

fade

burnt matches

i promised you a book

so i'll hold this pen

until the ink runs out

m.c

i thought i was putting her pieces

back together

but she is the one who

mended mine

The Goodbye

2

we said goodbye

and the silence

was so loud between us

you could hear my

thoughts say,

"please don't go"

burnt matches

i remember the sadness in your eyes

when you

asked me if i was alright

you said we needed to talk but i didn't

expect our final goodbyes

(more)

m.c

you were worth all the tears

that kept me up that night,

all the what ifs and could ofves

that ran through my mind

years from now

we will both be moved on

we'll know what's done is done

    - a girl you could never love

burnt matches

i'm on my knees

watching her leave

as i scream,

"please come back to me"

m.c

you asked me

what i missed the most

i paused then said,

"the part of me I left with you"

burnt matches

i won't beg you to stay

so i'll bite my tongue

when you walk away

m.c

i didn't care to lose anyone

until it was

you

burnt matches

i said,

"this is the last time you'd see me"

but that was before

i watched you walk

away

m.c

"almost" is somber

they almost fell in love

they almost were happy

burnt matches

pieces of me are missing

they are

with *her*

m.c

i couldn't keep you

so you'll be in these

lines

instead

burnt matches

you asked me how i've been without you,

my lips begin to quiver

do you mean how many bottles

of alcohol

i've been through in the last week?

or how i drive 100 mph

on the freeway

(more)

just to feel what i did the night you

kissed me?

or how I've replaced food

with a pack of cigarettes?

my voice shakes

but i continue to smile and say,

"I've been just fine"

burnt matches

each time someone loved her

she'd push them away

hell,

no one could make her stay

m.c

i wanted you

to be the main character in my

book

but you were only a few pages

The Regret

3

m.c

i saw the regret on your face

when we looked at each other

no words.

just regret

burnt matches

i promised myself

i would stop talking about

you to clean pages

but who stops admiring

the moon just because

it's too far away

m.c

the way she looked at me that day

i was willing to do anything

to make her stay

but she's

still the one who got away

burnt matches

and i'll never shed my soul that

way ever again

m.c

i drown myself in girls that

will never love me

but when i come up

for air,

you're all i see

burnt matches

"did you love her"

no but when

my fingertips

first touched *her*,

every atom in my body

ablazed like it never had before

"you loved her and still do"

m.c

you might not cross their mind tomorrow

but one day

they'll add too much cream

to their coffee

reminding them

of the color of your eyes

burnt matches

and if i've ever cared for you,

there's ink engraved

on pages with your name

written in the fonts

m.c

in another universe,

you want me

but i no longer want you

burnt matches

and if a blank page is a poem

that is the only one you

will ever

deserve

m.c

i spoke to the stars

about you last night

in hopes they will speak to you

you screamed back at them

but i'm asleep

i won't hear the stars say

"she misses you too"

burnt matches

we were like a movie

too good to be true

m.c

you weren't on my mind

when i kissed her

but then

i wished it was you

you weren't on my mind yesterday

but then

i heard the song we fell in love to

burnt matches

maybe in a parallel universe

our electrons

are infinite

in finding one another

m.c

i lost myself trying to find you

picking away your bad parts like spots on fruit

only to find myself crumbling

each time i'd

look for you

burnt matches

i knew it was over

when you fell asleep

without kissing me goodnight

- *the end of us*

you and i

were made up of endless lies

that covered an abundance of galaxies

but in that moment

we were nothing but beautiful

burnt matches

she's not the type to let

you look at her for too long

let alone touch her dreary soul

love is something she has never known

m.c

the shade of lipstick you would tell me

to take off

she adores

you hated the green shirt in the

back of my closet

now it's on her floor

burnt matches

i could see you thinking about

him when you touched

me

but here i am still

begging you to admire me

m.c

i started sleeping

in old t-shirts again

because that's what i wore before you

my life was majestic before you

and it'll be just as much

without you

burnt matches

it was oddly worthwhile to lose

you

to make this ink come alive again

m.c

i started writing poetry to make you

you love me

i haven't stopped since

you left me

i'll proceed until you come

back to me

burnt matches

you made my heart bleed

and you warned me before kissing me

that you would

but each time you'd look at me

it would resuscitate

forgetting how it felt once

before

Written by : Maylee Curtis
IG : @maylee_c1

Cover Illustrator : Dalton Vaughn
IG : @daltonvaughn

heartbreak inspired me

to write this much

www.ingramcontent.com/pod-product-compliance
Lightning Source LLC
LaVergne TN
LVHW041650060526
838200LV00040B/1789